THE HUMAN MACHINE

DIGESTION AND EXCRETION

Louise Spilsbury

Heinemann
LIBRARY

H www.heinemann.co.uk/library
Visit our website to find out more information about Heinemann Library books.

To order:

☎ Phone 44 (0)1865 888066

📄 Send a fax to 44 (0)1865 314091

💻 Visit the Heinemann Bookshop at www.heinemann.co.uk/library to browse our catalogue and order online.

First published in Great Britain by Heinemann, Halley Court, Jordan Hill, Oxford, OX2 8EJ, part of Harcourt Education.
Heinemann is a registered trademark of Harcourt Education Ltd.

Editorial: Nancy Dickmann and Rachel Howells
Design: Victoria Bevan and AMR Design Ltd
Illustrations: Medi-mation
Picture Research: Hannah Taylor
Production: Vicki Fitzgerald

Originated by Chroma
Printed and bound in China by CTPS
ISBN 978 0 431 19204 8 (hardback)

12 11 10 09 08
10 9 8 7 6 5 4 3 2 1

British Library Cataloguing in Publication Data
Spilsbury, Louise
Digestion and excretion. - (The human machine)
1. Digestion - Juvenile literature 2. Digestive organs - Juvenile literature
I. Title
612.3
A full catalogue record for this book is available from the British Library.

Acknowledgements
The publishers would like to thank the following for permission to reproduce photographs: ©Corbis pp. **9** (Royalty Free), **26** (Envision), **19** (Lester Lefkowitz), **16** (Roy Morsch), **10** (zefa/ Alexander Scott); ©Getty Images pp. **23**, **20** (Datacraft), **4** (Photodisc), **15** (Photographer's Choice), **5** (Stone +); ©iStockphoto p. **29** (Justin Horrocks), ©Masterfile p. **8** (John Lee); ©Photolibrary.com pp. **7**, **25** (Stockbyte); ©Science Photo Library pp. **27** (AJ Photo), **17** (Alex Bartel), **12** (Eye of Science), **28** (Roger Harris).

Cover photograph of transparent male body containing the digestive system reproduced with permission of ©Getty Images/ 3D4Medical.com.

The publishers would like to thank David Wright for his assistance in the preparation of this book.

Every effort has been made to contact copyright holders of any material reproduced in this book. Any omissions will be rectified in subsequent printings if notice is given to the publishers.

Contents

What is digestion?   4

What are the parts of the digestive system?   6

How is food digested?   8

How does the body use food?   16

What happens to food waste?   20

How can we keep the digestive system healthy?   26

The world's most complex machine   28

Glossary   30

Find out more   31

Index   32

Any words appearing in the text in bold, **like this**, are explained in the glossary.

What is digestion?

The human body is often described as a complex machine, made up of many different parts that work together. To make machines work, you need a source of **energy**. Computers and MP3 players run on electricity, and cars and aeroplanes run on petrol or diesel fuel. The human machine runs on a variety of different food fuels, including breads and pasta, fruits and vegetables, and meats, nuts, and cheese.

Digesting food

The body cannot use the food we take into our mouths as it is. To use food your body must first digest it, or break it down. Inside the body, the different parts of the digestive system process the food. They break it down until it **dissolves** into incredibly tiny bits in liquid. The **nutrients** in this liquid give the human machine the energy it needs to live. They also supply the raw materials the body uses to grow and repair any damage.

Today some cars run on ethanol, a kind of fuel made from corn oil, so the same corn plants can be used to run vehicles as well as human engines!

We cook some types of food, such as spaghetti, to make them easier for the body to digest. Cooking also changes the taste and appearance of food.

Waste not, want not

Some of the parts of the food we take in are not useful and could even be bad for us. The excretory system helps us to stay healthy by **excreting** (forcing out) wastes that could build up and make us sick. Unwanted parts of food and other food wastes pass from the digestive system to the excretory system and out of the body. After you have eaten a meal your body is hard at work processing that fuel for up to 24 hours. The food passes through many different body parts on its long journey!

FAVOURITE PLANT FOODS

There are more than 50,000 different plants that people can eat. However, just three of them – rice, maize (corn), and wheat – provide 60 percent of the world's food energy intake! People grow fields of these plants all around the world and often eat them for most meals. However, they do not provide all the nutrients people need.

What are the parts of the digestive system?

The digestive system is rather like a conveyor belt in a factory. It consists mostly of a long tube made of several different **organs**. (Organs are body parts with a particular job to do.) This long tube is called the **alimentary canal**. Food passing through this tube is processed and sorted into useful nutrients the body wants and waste it does not want. It is a bit like the way a juicing machine separates out the part of the fruit you can drink.

The stomach

From the mouth, food passes down the throat into the **oesophagus**. The oesophagus is a soft, **muscular** tube that is up to 30 centimetres (12 inches) long. It moves food to the stomach. The stomach is an organ that is rather like a stretchy bag. It holds up to 1 litre (2 pints) of food a person has recently eaten. The stomach is about 15 centimetres (6 inches) wide at its widest point.

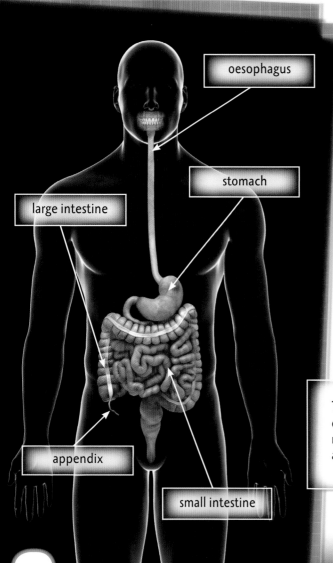

oesophagus

stomach

large intestine

appendix

small intestine

This is the alimentary canal. It is mostly coiled up but if stretched out would measure 9 metres (30 feet) long in an adult. That's the length of a large bus!

The digestive system works a bit like this juicing machine. It allows the body to separate off the parts of food that are good for us, such as apple juice, from the waste we do not want, such as pips and skin.

The intestines

From the stomach, the partly digested food passes into the **small intestine**. This coiled, narrow tube makes up around two-thirds of the total length of the alimentary canal. It is where most digestion occurs. Undigested food and some water travels to the **large intestine**, which breaks down food remains and then passes waste out of the **anus**.

A SPARE PART

Our digestive system has an extra bit on the large intestine called the appendix. Scientists think that in the past the appendix might have helped humans to digest tough, woody plant foods. Today it does not have a particular job as we eat more cooked foods. Therefore, if it gets infected it is sometimes removed altogether.

How is food digested?

The process of digestion starts before you take your first bite of food. When you see a dish of delicious dinner or smell something simmering in the kitchen, your salivary glands start to work. The salivary glands are under the tongue. They produce saliva, or spit, which moistens food and makes it softer. Saliva also contains **enzymes**, chemicals that start to break the food down.

Tongue tactics

Your tongue is another part of the human machine that helps with digestion. It moves food around your mouth to spread the saliva. It also moves the food towards the back teeth so they can grind up the food. The tongue is covered in taste buds. Taste buds do an important job in digestion by warning us if food is "off", as well as letting us taste food flavours.

The expression "makes your mouth water" is not far wrong because the sight and smell of food does stimulate your salivary glands!

incisors

molars

canines

If you run your tongue over your teeth you should be able to feel the different shapes of these vital tools.

Biting and chewing

Your teeth are like different tools. They are different shapes because they have different jobs to do. The four front teeth are incisors. They have straight, flat ends that bite through food so we can take a piece into our mouths. On each side of the incisors are long, sharp, and pointed canine teeth that grip and tear off pieces of tough food. At the back of your mouth are wide, flat-topped molars. These teeth are used for crushing, grinding, and chewing.

CHEMICAL DEMOLITION GANGS

Enzymes in the saliva start to digest **carbohydrates**. Carbohydrates are foods such as cereals, potatoes, breads, and pasta. The enzymes soak into the food and change the surface so it starts to break up into pieces of **glucose**. Glucose is a kind of sugar, which is why bread starts to taste a little sweet after you've been chewing it for a few minutes.

Swallowing

Together, the teeth and tongue shape the chewed food into a ball. Then you use your throat to swallow the ball. The throat is made of two pipes. The oesophagus takes food to the stomach and the trachea takes air to the **lungs**. A flap of skin called the **epiglottis** normally closes like a trapdoor to make sure food only goes into the oesophagus. If the epiglottis doesn't have enough time to close, food gets into the trachea. This makes you automatically choke or cough to clear the airway.

WHY SHOULD I CLEAN MY TEETH?

When we chew food, especially sweet, sticky food, some of it coats our teeth. **Microscopic** living things called **bacteria** that live in the mouth feed on sugars on teeth. They form a thin, tough layer there called plaque. Bacteria in plaque change the sugars into **acid**. Acid is a strong chemical. It can make holes called cavities in teeth, which need to be filled. Cleaning your teeth gets rid of the plaque.

You should try to clean your teeth for at least two minutes, three times a day after meals.

Muscles in action

The walls of the alimentary canal have muscles all the way along them. These muscles squeeze the food through the oesophagus after it leaves the throat. The food moves along the tube rather as toothpaste does when you squeeze the tube. The muscles in the oesophagus are quite strong and they can keep your food going in the right direction even if you eat upside down – although this is not to be recommended!

Into the stomach

When food passes into the stomach, a ring of muscle at the end of the oesophagus squeezes tight to stop the food getting out again. When you swallow food or liquid, you also swallow air into the stomach. The air we breathe contains gases that you need to get rid of. This gas is sometimes forced out of the stomach, up through the oesophagus, and out of your mouth as a burp.

The muscle action used to move food along the oesophagus is called peristalsis.

Muscles in the oesophagus contract (tighten) behind food, pushing it along

Food gradually moves through the oesophagus

The food processor

The stomach is like a food processor that turns lumps of food into a mushy mixture called **chyme**. The walls of the stomach have strong muscles that squeeze and churn the food inside, mixing and mashing it together. The stomach walls also release gastric juice. This contains strong acids to kill bacteria in food we have eaten that could otherwise make us sick. It also contains enzymes to break down **proteins**. Digestion in the stomach takes up to six hours, depending on the types of foods we have eaten. For example, it takes longer to digest meat than bread.

Into the small intestine

Chyme moves from the stomach into the small intestine through a small flap. It then stays in the small intestine for about four hours while it is digested some more. The small intestine is only about 2.5 centimetres (1 inch) wide. It is lined with thousands of microscopic **villi**, tiny folds that look like fingers. They stick out of the walls of the small intestine, pointing towards the centre.

Villi can only be seen through a microscope. They help us to quickly absorb the nutrients available in the food we have eaten.

The value of villi

Inside the villi there are tiny blood vessels called capillaries. The **vitamins** and nutrients from the digested food in the small intestine pass through the villi into these capillaries. The villi greatly increase the total area of the intestine walls, so a large amount of nutrients can be absorbed at a time. Once nutrients have passed into the blood, they can be carried around the body to where they are needed.

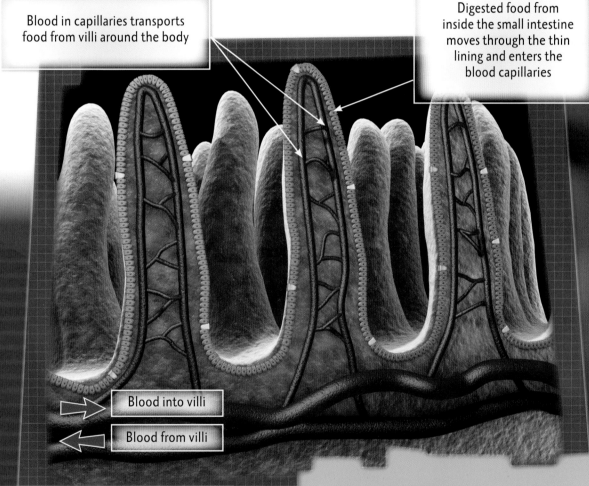

Blood in capillaries transports food from villi around the body

Digested food from inside the small intestine moves through the thin lining and enters the blood capillaries

Blood into villi

Blood from villi

Just inside each of the villi are tiny blood vessels. The blood vessels absorb nutrients that pass through the thin surface of the villi. The yellow **cells** make mucus (slime) that helps the food move through the intestine.

WHY DOES MY STOMACH RUMBLE?

Your stomach rumbles if it churns around when there is not much food in it. This causes the gases inside to make a gurgling sound. The stomach is usually empty after six hours, although you might feel hungry before then!

Aids to digestion

Food does not pass through the **liver**, **gall bladder**, or **pancreas** while it is being digested, but these organs are important tools in the digestive system. The liver and pancreas produce substances such as enzymes that help to break down food. The gall bladder acts as a storage warehouse for some of these substances.

The basics about bile

The liver is an organ about the width of your rib cage. One of its jobs is to produce bile. Bile is a greenish-yellow digestive juice that helps to break up fatty foods. The liver stores the bile in the gall bladder, a pear-shaped organ found just below the liver. When the body needs bile for digestion, for example after you have eaten, the gall bladder squirts some into the small intestine.

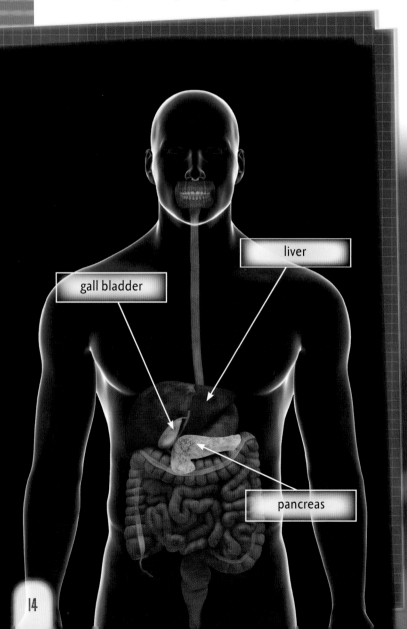

gall bladder

liver

pancreas

The liver, pancreas, and gall bladder supply the small intestine with the liquids it needs to digest food fully.

Pancreatic juice

The pancreas is about 18 centimetres (7 inches) long and lies behind and just below the stomach. The pancreas makes pancreatic juice. When you eat, your pancreas releases this juice into the first part of your small intestine. The fluid contains enzymes that break down fats, proteins, and carbohydrates.

When you wash the dishes, soap and detergent change oily food into tiny droplets that can be broken down and washed away more easily. Bile works on fatty food in a similar way.

WHY DO PEOPLE VOMIT?

If you have harmful bacteria in your stomach or intestine when you are ill, or you eat food with lots of strong chemicals in it, you may vomit to get rid of it. The muscles in your stomach and intestines automatically push the food up your oesophagus and out of your mouth. Vomit usually tastes bitter because it contains bile and gastric juices.

How does the body use food?

From the villi, blood carries nutrients to the liver through tubes called blood vessels. The liver is the largest organ inside your body and it works like a chemical-processing factory.

Life in the liver

After a meal, the liver sorts out the nutrients. It converts useful nutrients into substances your body can use to make the energy it needs. The liver is also a storage depot. It holds on to nutrients and vitamins until supplies get low. Then it releases them back into the blood to be distributed around the body. For example, your body cannot use all the glucose it produces at once, so the liver stores it as a substance called glycogen. The liver changes this back to glucose when the body needs it. It is a bit like the way a battery stores energy, releasing it only when it is needed by an electrical machine.

When you use up a lot of energy, your liver releases nutrients into the blood so your body can make more energy.

At a waste recycling centre, magnets sort out useful metals from waste materials. In the human machine the liver sorts out the useful chemicals from the harmful or useless ones in blood.

Waste filter

Digested food also contains substances your body does not need. As well as sorting and storing nutrients, the liver also acts as a waste disposal unit. It helps to clean the blood, for example, by turning harmful substances into bile. In total, an adult's liver dumps around half a litre (1 pint) of bile into the gall bladder each day.

JAUNDICE

When a person has jaundice, their eyes and skin look a bit yellow. This happens because there is a build-up of waste products such as bile in their blood. It is a sign that something is wrong with their liver. The liver is a vital organ, so a doctor should always check any sign of jaundice.

Delivery service

When the liver has sorted the digested food and disposed of the waste, the blood acts like a fleet of delivery trucks. It carries nutrients to all of the different living **cells** in your body. Each one of us is made up of hundreds of millions of cells, which is why cells are often called the building blocks of living things.

How do cells use nutrients?

The cells of the body use different nutrients in different ways. For example, during the process of digestion, proteins from foods such as milk and cheese are broken down into their separate parts, called amino acids. The cells combine these different amino acids in different ways to build new cells and to repair damaged ones. Most of the carbohydrates we digest form glucose, and cells use glucose to make energy.

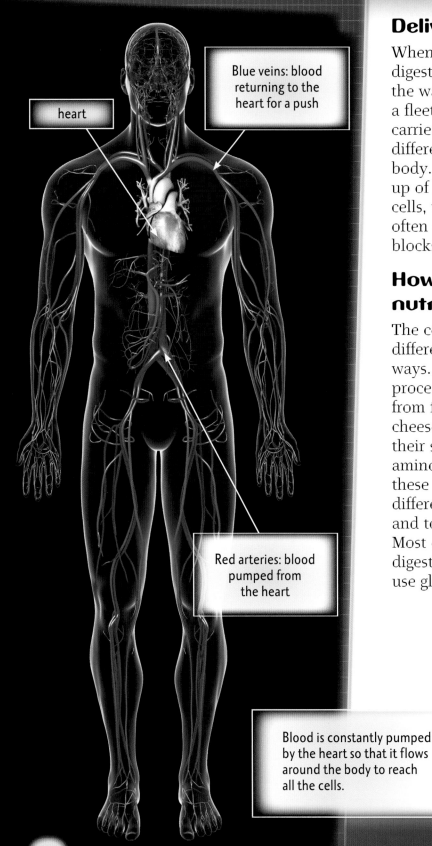

heart

Blue veins: blood returning to the heart for a push

Red arteries: blood pumped from the heart

Blood is constantly pumped by the heart so that it flows around the body to reach all the cells.

Collecting waste products

Complicated chemical reactions take place inside individual cells when they use up nutrients. These reactions produce some waste in the cells. For example, ammonia is the waste that is left over when cells use proteins to make new cells. Ammonia is toxic (poisonous) in large quantities. The blood carries ammonia away from the cells and back through the circulation system until it reaches the liver. The liver then changes the ammonia into a different waste, called **urea**, which is less harmful to the body.

In some ways blood cells are like lorries on a winding system of roads. They travel around the body in blood vessels, dropping off nutrients to cells and collecting waste.

RELEASING ENERGY

Inside individual cells, oxygen combines with glucose in a special reaction to release energy. Any substance that combines with oxygen to release heat energy is called a fuel. In a bonfire the fuel is wood, but in a cell it is glucose. In a cell there are no flames as in a bonfire, but some heat is produced.

What happens to food waste?

Kidneys are organs that are part of the body's waste disposal, or excretory, system. We have two kidneys, each about the size of a fist and shaped like a kidney bean. When blood passes through the kidneys, the kidneys remove excess water and waste products from the blood. The kidneys work fast—all of the blood in your body passes through your kidneys in four minutes.

How do kidneys work?

Uncleaned blood comes into each kidney through a large blood vessel. Kidneys work by filtering or straining waste from the blood. The filtering units inside the kidneys are called nephrons. Nephrons are rather like tiny tubes, and each kidney has a million of them! After waste has been removed, the cleaned blood leaves the kidney and re-enters the circulation system.

A coffee machine removes the unwanted grains of coffee from the liquid. The kidneys remove unwanted waste from the blood in a similar way.

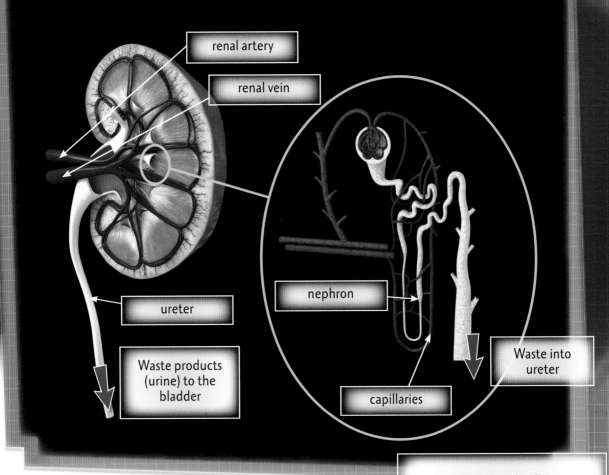

renal artery

renal vein

ureter

nephron

Waste products (urine) to the bladder

capillaries

Waste into ureter

Filtering fluids

A tiny blood vessel called a capillary winds around the inside of each of the cup-shaped nephrons in a kidney. As blood passes through each capillary, waste and some useful substances filter into the nephron. Nutrients such as glucose then move back into the capillary, along with most of the water. These vital substances flow on through the capillaries, to the renal vein, and out of the kidney.

In this picture the dirty blood entering the kidney is coloured red. The cleaned blood, leaving the kidney through the renal vein, is coloured blue.

WHAT IS DIALYSIS?

When a person's kidneys are damaged, a dialysis machine can be used to clean the blood and remove waste and excess water. A dialysis machine filters blood using an artificial filter. A tube is attached to a needle that has been inserted into a blood vessel in the arm. Blood travels from the body to the machine, is cleaned, and then returns to the body through a second tube.

Waste disposal

The kidneys combine the different waste collected by the nephrons, such as urea, with excess water from the blood. This forms urine. Urine trickles out of the kidneys through two narrow tubes called ureters and passes into the bladder.

What is the bladder?

The bladder is a stretchy pouch that is used as a storage tank for urine. When it is empty, the bladder has many folds. These folds open up and flatten out as the bladder fills up, allowing it to expand. An adult bladder can usually hold about half a litre (one pint) before it feels uncomfortable. Urine leaves the body by flowing out of the bladder and down a tube called the urethra. The urethral sphincter is a ring of muscle at the point where the bladder and urethra meet. It is usually closed to hold urine in the bladder.

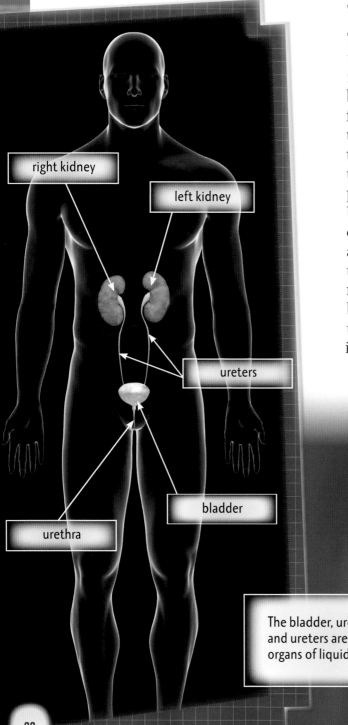

right kidney

left kidney

ureters

bladder

urethra

The bladder, urethra, and ureters are the main organs of liquid excretion.

How does the bladder work?

When the bladder is stretched to a certain point – usually about half full – **nerves** in the bladder wall send a message to the brain telling it that the bladder needs emptying. Nerves are like telephone wires inside the human body. They carry messages to and from the brain. The brain sends a message back, telling the body it is time to urinate. When you are ready, you relax the sphincter and urine flows down the urethra and out of your body.

We also get rid of some waste when we sweat. Sweat helps us cool down and it also releases small amounts of the waste that is carried by the blood.

WHAT IS SWEAT?

We sweat to cool down. When sweat dries from our body, it takes away some of the warmth too. Sweat also helps to carry waste from the body. Although it consists mostly of water, sweat also contains some urea and salt that is filtered from the blood as the blood travels under the skin.

Solid waste

Some of the materials in food cannot be digested in the small intestine. For example, some parts of fruits and vegetables are made of **fibre**, a tough substance that does not contain any nutrients. Fibre, other bits of undigested food, and used bile pass straight from the small intestine into the large intestine.

In the large intestine

The large intestine, or bowel, is made up of three sections: the colon, rectum, and anus. The first and largest part is the colon. Undigested food stays in the colon for up to 24 hours. During this time most of the remaining water is removed from the waste. The semi-solid waste that is left over is called faeces.

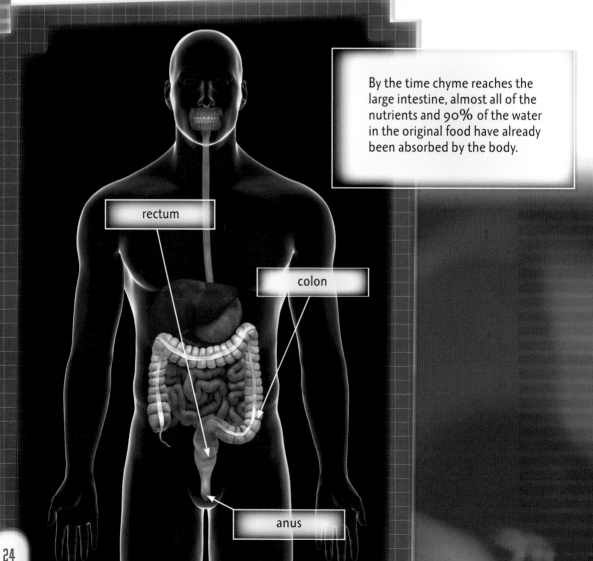

By the time chyme reaches the large intestine, almost all of the nutrients and 90% of the water in the original food have already been absorbed by the body.

rectum

colon

anus

Dumping the waste

Some bacteria normally live in the colon. They break down some of the fibre to nourish themselves. This makes the faeces easier to get rid of. Mucus made by cells lining the colon help the faeces slip through the colon into the rectum. Faeces are stored in the rectum until we are ready to pass them out in stools that leave the body through the anus.

We sometimes also pass gas from the anus. This gas is created in the alimentary canal when food is broken down and when bacteria in the colon break down undigested fibre.

Many yoghurts contain probiotics. Probiotics can help keep our digestive system, particularly the large intestine, healthy.

FRIENDLY BACTERIA?

There is a mix of healthy and harmful bacteria in your colon. Many doctors suggest eating food such as yoghurt that contains probiotics. These are healthy or "friendly" bacteria. They help maintain a healthy colon by increasing the numbers of helpful bacteria there.

How can we keep the digestive system healthy?

To keep your digestive system healthy you need to eat a balance of healthy foods and drink plenty of water. Your body is mostly made of water, and water keeps food moving through the digestive system smoothly. You lose water every day, through sweat and urination, and it is important to replace that supply.

Different food groups

You need to eat food from different food groups. Fruits and vegetables and grains such as rice or wheat supply us with carbohydrates and also with much of the fibre and vitamins we need. Try to eat at least five portions of fruit or vegetables each day.

Carbohydrates in cereals, bread, or pasta made from grains or in potatoes take longer to digest than those in sweet foods. They therefore release energy gradually and let us remain active over a long time. So fill up on the right carbohydrates at mealtimes and not biscuits or cakes in between.

Wholemeal carbohydrates like this loaf of bread contain lots of fibre. Fibre keeps our digestive system healthy by helping to push waste through the alimentary canal.

You should try to eat a portion of protein with at least two of your main meals each day. Protein is found in meat, fish, and pulses such as lentils. The other food groups are dairy foods such as milk and cheese, and oily foods such as nuts and seeds. These supply some protein but mostly fat. This nutrient is important for keeping us healthy, but in large amounts it can make us overweight and unfit.

Minerals, such as calcium and iron, are also vital for your health. For example, calcium builds strong bones and teeth. You should get the minerals you need by eating different foods from all food groups.

You can help your digestive system by eating healthy foods in the correct amount and also by washing your hands to keep germs out.

WHY SHOULD I WASH MY HANDS?

It is especially important to wash your hands with warm, soapy water after going to the toilet because you may have traces of faeces or urine on your fingers. If the bacteria in these waste substances get into your mouth and back into your system they could make you ill.

The world's most complex machine

The human body is often described as the world's most complex machine, but of course it is not really a machine at all. Machines are non-living, mechanical objects, whereas our bodies are natural, living things. But there are similarities. Like a machine, the body is made up of different parts that work together in systems to do particular jobs. These different systems work together to make the whole body – or the human machine – run smoothly and efficiently.

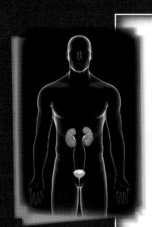

THE SKELETAL SYSTEM

This system of bones supports the other parts of the body, rather as the metal frame of a car supports the vehicle.

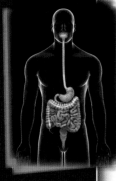

THE DIGESTIVE SYSTEM

The digestive system works as a food-processing machine. It consists of various organs that work together to break down food into forms that the body can use as fuel and raw materials.

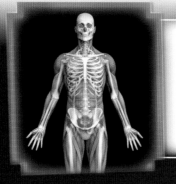

THE EXCRETORY SYSTEM

This is the human machine's waste disposal system, removing harmful substances and waste produced by the other parts of the body.

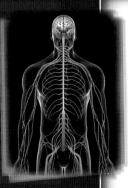

THE NERVOUS SYSTEM

This is the human machine's communication and control system. The brain transmits and receives messages from the senses and the rest of the body. It does this through a network of nerves connected to the brain via the spinal cord.

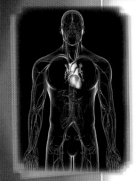

THE CIRCULATORY SYSTEM

This is the body's delivery system. The heart pumps blood through blood vessels, carrying nutrients and oxygen to the other parts and removing waste from cells.

THE RESPIRATORY SYSTEM

This system provides the rest of the body with the oxygen it needs to get energy from food. It also releases waste gases from the body into the air.

THE MUSCULAR SYSTEM

Muscles are the human machine's motors. Some muscles make the bones of the skeleton move; others work as pumps to keep substances moving through the body.

Glossary

acid type of substance. Mild acids such as lemon juice taste sharp, but strong acids, such as the acid made in our stomachs, damage or break down other substances.

alimentary canal passage that food moves along during digestion, from mouth to anus

anus hole at the end of the large intestine through which waste solids and gas leave the body

bacteria microscopic living thing. Some bacteria can cause disease.

bile digestive juice made by the liver that digests fat in the small intestine

capillary smallest kind of blood vessel in the body

carbohydrate kinds of foods such as pasta, bread, and potatoes that give us energy

cell building block or basic unit of all living things. The human body is made up of millions of different cells.

chyme paste of partly digested food in the stomach

digest break down foods we eat

dissolve disintegrate or disappear into a liquid such as water

energy in science, energy is the ability to do work—to move, grow, change, or to do anything else that living things do

enzyme special protein that helps body processes including digestion

epiglottis flap behind the tongue which stops food going towards the lungs as you swallow

excrete force out waste

fibre tough substance, found in some foods, which the body cannot digest

gall bladder pouch near the liver that stores bile

glucose kind of sugar that the body obtains from carbohydrate foods such as pasta and potatoes

kidney organ that filters waste from the blood and forms urine

large intestine (also called the bowel) part of the alimentary tract, made up of the colon, rectum, and anus

liver large organ that removes and stores nutrients and converts some waste in the blood into bile

lungs organs we use to breathe with

microscopic substance so small that you need a microscope to see it

mineral non-living substance such as metal, salt, sand, or calcium.Minerals often come from the earth.

mucus slimy substance made by some cells. Mucus is found throughout the alimentary canal.

muscle tissue in the body that contracts (tightens) to cause movement

muscular made of muscle

nerve thin strand that carries messages between the brain and the rest of the body

nutrient substance that plants and animals need to grow and survive

oesophagus tube between throat and stomach

organ part of the body that performs a specific function

pancreas organ that makes enzymes used in digestion

protein type of nutrient found in foods. Meat is a protein and is vital for the growth and repair of the body.

small intestine part of the alimentary canal between the stomach and large intestine

urea waste product created by liver after cells use up proteins

villi tiny finger-shaped folds inside the small intestine

vitamins important nutrients released after our bodies digest foods such as fruits and vegetables

Find out more

Websites

At www.kidshealth.org/kid/body/digest_SW.html you will find "The Real Deal on the Digestive System". The kidshealth website also has useful sections on nutrients and many different human body topics.

At http://exhibits.pacsci.org/nutrition/nutrition_cafe.html you can learn more about eating the right foods to stay healthy by playing some games.

At http://vilenski.org/science/humanbody/hb_html/digestivesystem.html you can view the digestive system as part of the "Human Body Adventure." Click to see close-up views of different parts of the digestive system.

Books

Digestion, Steve Parker (Hodder Wayland, 2004)

Eating Properly, Jonathan Rees (Franklin Watts, 2004)

Guts: Our Digestive System, Seymour Simon (Harper Collins, 2006)

The Human Body: The Digestive System, Susan Glass (Perfection Learning, 2004)

Index

acids 10, 12, 18
alimentary canal 6, 7, 11,
    25, 26
amino acids 18
ammonia 19
anus 7, 24
appendix 6, 7
arteries 18, 21

bacteria 10, 12, 15, 25, 27
bile 14, 15, 17, 24
bladder 22, 23
blood 16, 17, 18, 19, 20
blood cells 19
blood vessels 13, 16, 21
bowel see large intestine
brains 23
burping 11

capillaries 13, 21
carbohydrates 9, 15, 18, 26
cells 13, 18, 19
    blood cells 19
    repair 18
choking 10
chyme 12, 24
circulatory system 18, 19, 29
colon 24, 25

dialysis 21
digestive system 4, 6-19,
    26, 28

energy 4, 16, 18, 19, 26
enzymes 8, 9, 12, 14, 15
epiglottis 10
ethanol 4
excretory system 5, 20-5, 28
    see also waste products

faeces 24, 25, 27
fats 15, 27
fibre 24, 25, 26
food and diet 4, 5, 26-7
    cooking 5
flavours 8
food groups 26-7
    plant foods 5

gallbladder 14, 17
gases 11, 13, 25
gastric juice 12, 15
glucose 9, 16, 18, 19, 21
glycogen 16

hands, washing 27
heart 18

jaundice 17

kidneys 20-1, 22

large intestine 6, 7, 24
liver 14, 16, 17, 18, 19
lungs 10

machines 4, 28
minerals 27
mucus 13, 25
muscles 6, 11, 12, 15, 22
muscular system 29

nephrons 20, 21, 22
nerves 23
nervous system 29
nutrients 4, 6, 12, 13, 16,
    17, 18, 19

oesophagus 6, 11, 14
organs 6, 14
oxygen 19

pancreas 14, 15
pancreatic juice 15
peristalsis 11
plaque 10
probiotics 25
proteins 12, 15, 18, 27

rectum 24, 25
respiratory system 29
rumbling stomach 13

saliva 8, 9
salivary glands 8
salt 23
skeletal system 28
small intentine 6, 7, 12, 13, 24
stomach 6, 10, 11, 12, 13
swallowing 10
sweat 23, 26

taste buds 8
teeth 9, 10
    canines 9
    cleaning 10
    incisors 9
    molars 9
throat 10
tongue 8
trachea 10

urea 19, 22, 23
ureters 21
urethra 22, 23
urethral sphincter 22, 23
urine 21, 22, 23, 26, 27

veins 18, 21
villi 12, 13, 16
vitamins 13, 26
vomiting 15

waste products 5, 7, 17, 19,
    20-5, 26
water 20, 22, 23, 24, 26